AUTHOR

Luca Stefano Cristini is an Italian historian and historical illustrator. He currently lives near Bergamo in northern Italy. A son of art, his father was a well-known painter and student of Mario Sironi and Achille Funi. Great expert, enthusiast and experimenter of Digital Graphic art in all its forms and technologies. Luca's painting style and technique is utterly flawless and beautiful, rich in detail and texture. In his works he signs himself KL.

PUBLISHING'S NOTE

None of **unpublished** images or text of our book may be reproduced in any format without the expressed written permission of LCE publisher when not indicate as marked with license creative commons 3.0 or 4.0. in any case for our graphic works in the *Full-Cube* series, our artists, by whatever means they work: traditional, manually, digitally Pphotoshop and/or various other regualr programs for doing illustrative graphics) make ethical and conscious use of the rights of artists (current contemporaries or those who have been deceased for more than 70 years), we avoid references to contemporary and active artists and in any case we elaborate complex styles and training procedures that are the result of our artists' graphic elaboration according to their personal taste and style. The publisher remains to disposition of the possible having right for all the doubtful sources images or not identifies.

ACKNOWLEDGMENTS

A special thanks to to all the friends, artists and outsiders who helped us in this adventure..

Title: **NYC AMAZING VIEWS OF THE BIG APPLE** by Luca S. Cristini
First edition by Luca Cristini Editore February 2024
Cover & Art Design: Luca S. Cristini. ISBN code: 9791255890737
Published by Luca Cristini Editore (LCE Publisher), via Orio 33/D- 24050 Zanica (BG) ITALY.
Code.: **FULL-CUBE 003**, Editorial series code: **FC003 SILENT BOOK**

NYC Flatiron Building

CONTENTS

NYC

MITH AND IMAGES OF THE GREAT APPLE

LUCA STEFANO CRISTINI

FULL CUBE

BOOK TO COLLECT

New York City and the Age of Jazz

The crazy, Dystopic, baroque, Surreal, Amazing Big Apple

New York in the 1930s and during the Jazz Age was a vibrant and dynamic city, where culture, art, and entertainment flourished. It was the setting of many famous works of literature, music, and cinema, such as The Great Gatsby by F. Scott Fitzgerald, Rhapsody in Blue by George Gershwin, and Anything Goes by Cole Porter. The most important features of New York in this era were:

◆ The skyscrapers: New York was home to some of the tallest and most iconic buildings in the world, such as the Empire State Building, the Chrysler Building, and the Rockefeller Center. These skyscrapers symbolized the economic and technological progress of the city, as well as its ambition and glamour.

◆ The streets: New York was a bustling and crowded metropolis, where people from different backgrounds and walks of life mingled and interacted. The streets were filled with cars, taxis, buses, and pedestrians, creating a lively and chaotic atmosphere. The streets also offered various attractions and distractions, such as theaters, cinemas, shops, restaurants, and nightclubs.

◆ The jazz clubs: New York was the epicenter of the jazz scene, where some of the most talented and influential musicians performed and recorded. Jazz was a new and innovative style of music that combined elements of blues, ragtime, and folk music, and featured improvisation, syncopation, and complex rhythms. Some of the famous jazz clubs in New York were the Cotton Club, the Savoy Ballroom, and the Village Vanguard. Some of the legendary jazz artists who played in New York were Duke Ellington, Louis Armstrong, Billie Holiday, and Charlie Parker.

◆ The speakeasies: New York was also the center of the prohibition era, where the sale and consumption of alcohol was banned by law. However, this did not stop people from drinking and partying, as they resorted to secret and illegal bars called speakeasies. Speakeasies were hidden behind fake fronts, such as bookstores, restaurants, or laundries, and required passwords or invitations to enter. Speakeasies were often raided by the police or the mob, adding to the thrill and danger of the experience. Some of the notorious speakeasies in New York were the Back Room, the 21 Club, and Chumley's.

◆ The flappers: New York was also the scene of a social and cultural revolution, where a new generation of women emerged and challenged the traditional norms and expectations of femininity. Flappers were young women who wore short dresses, bobbed hair, and makeup, and who smoked, drank, danced, and dated freely. Flappers expressed their independence, freedom, and rebellion, and became the icons of the Jazz Age. Some of the famous flappers in New York were Zelda Fitzgerald, Clara Bow, and Josephine Baker.

New York is a city of contrasts, where the old and the new, the real and the imaginary, the sublime and the grotesque, coexist and collide. Imagine a New York where:

◆ The modern skyscrapers are adorned with baroque and rococo portals, creating a striking contrast between the sleek glass and steel and the elaborate stone and wood. The portals are carved with intricate motifs of angels, flowers, shells, and scrolls, inviting you to enter a different world beyond the facade. Some of the portals are functional, leading to offices, apartments, or hotels, while others are purely decorative, hiding nothing but empty walls or dark alleys.

◆ The dystopian traffic is a constant challenge and a source of stress for the inhabitants and visitors of the city. The streets are jammed with cars, buses, trucks, bikes, and pedestrians, honking, shouting, and weaving their way through the chaos. The air is polluted with smog and noise, and the sidewalks are littered with trash and graffiti. The traffic lights are often broken or ignored, and the rules of the road are flexible and negotiable. Accidents and road rage are common, and the police are overwhelmed and underpaid.

◆ The wonderful people are the soul and the spice of the city. They are diverse, colorful, creative, and resilient. They come from all over the world, bringing their cultures, languages, cuisines, and stories. They are artists, musicians, writers, actors, dancers, and dreamers. They are entrepreneurs, workers, students, teachers, and activists. They are friendly, helpful, generous, and optimistic. They are also rude, impatient, selfish, and cynical. They are complex, contradictory, and fascinating. They are New York.

And now enjoy our silent book

BIRD'S EYE VIEW

THE STREETS AND TRAFFIC

Locations, places and buildings

MACY'S   MACY'S

NYC MAGIC AND ABSURD

CRISTINI EDITORE
FULL CUBE